# Black Holes to the Oort Cloud

## Beyond Our Solar System Cosmology for Kids

### Children's Cosmology Books

Copyright 2016

All Rights reserved. No part of this book may be reproduced or used in any way or form or by any means whether electronic or mechanical, this means that you cannot record or photocopy any material ideas or tips that are provided in this book

Kids let's learn about really big stuff: like black holes and the Oort Cloud.

Most of us know our planet is part of a solar system, and our solar system is part of a galaxy with a huge number of other systems more or less like our own.

# What are Black Holes?

These are strange fascinating objects. They are found in outer space.

Black holes have strong gravitational attraction. A black hole is a region in which the gravitational field is more powerful than anything else. Everything that comes near it cannot escape from its grasp. That even includes light.

Black holes are strange objects with extreme density. They are more massive than anything else we know of.

Even nearby stars can be captured by a black hole's strong gravitational pull. Over time, the galaxy changes as some solar systems get swallowed by black holes.

Black holes are found in between galaxies. There may be billions of them in the space, but the nearest one is very far from us.

Black holes cover only a small region despite their huge mass.

Because their strong gravitational pull affects even light, scientists find it difficult to see them.

# What is the Oort Cloud?

The Oort Cloud is an immense spherical cloud. It surrounds our solar system, beyond the planets like Earth and Jupiter. There are perhaps trillions of objects within the Oort Cloud. They are called Trans-Neptunian Objects, and some may be as big as the planets we already know.

The two parts of the Oort Cloud are the inner cloud, which resembles a disc, and the outer cloud, which is more like a sphere.

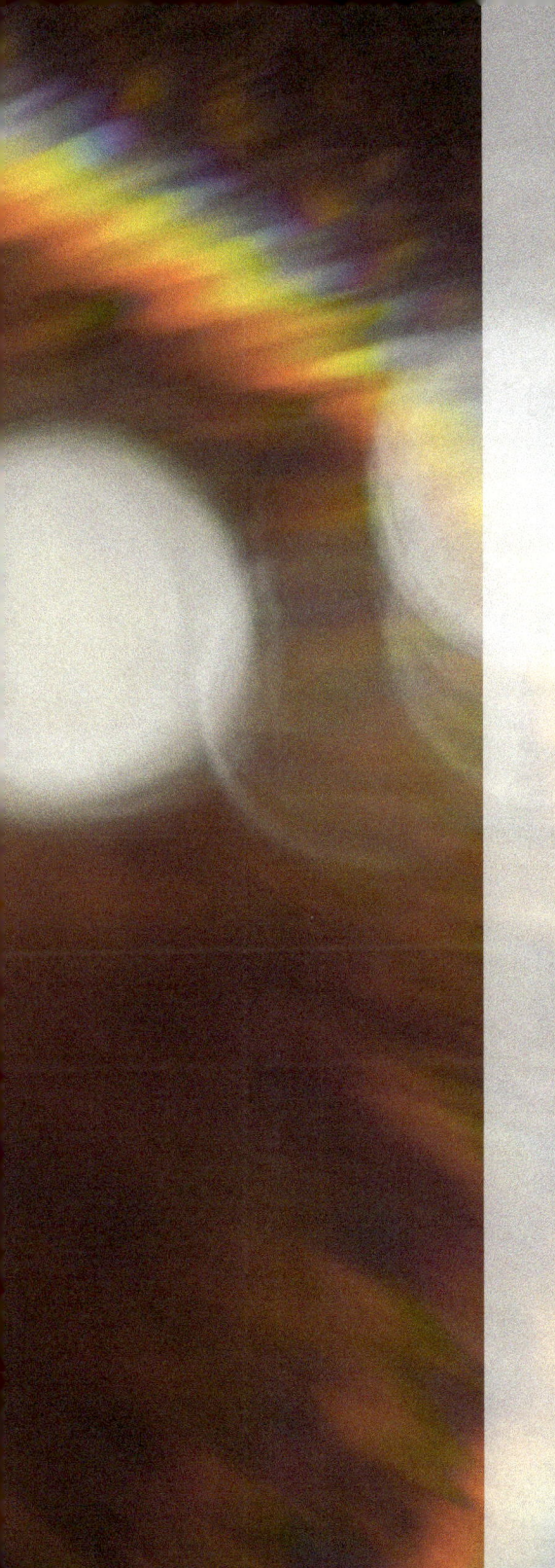

The Oort Cloud is like a shell of icy objects, going around our sun but not getting much warmth from it.

The Oort Cloud was discovered in 1950 by a Dutch astronomer, Jan Oort. The cloud is named after him. It is so far from us that not even the Voyager space craft has reached it yet.

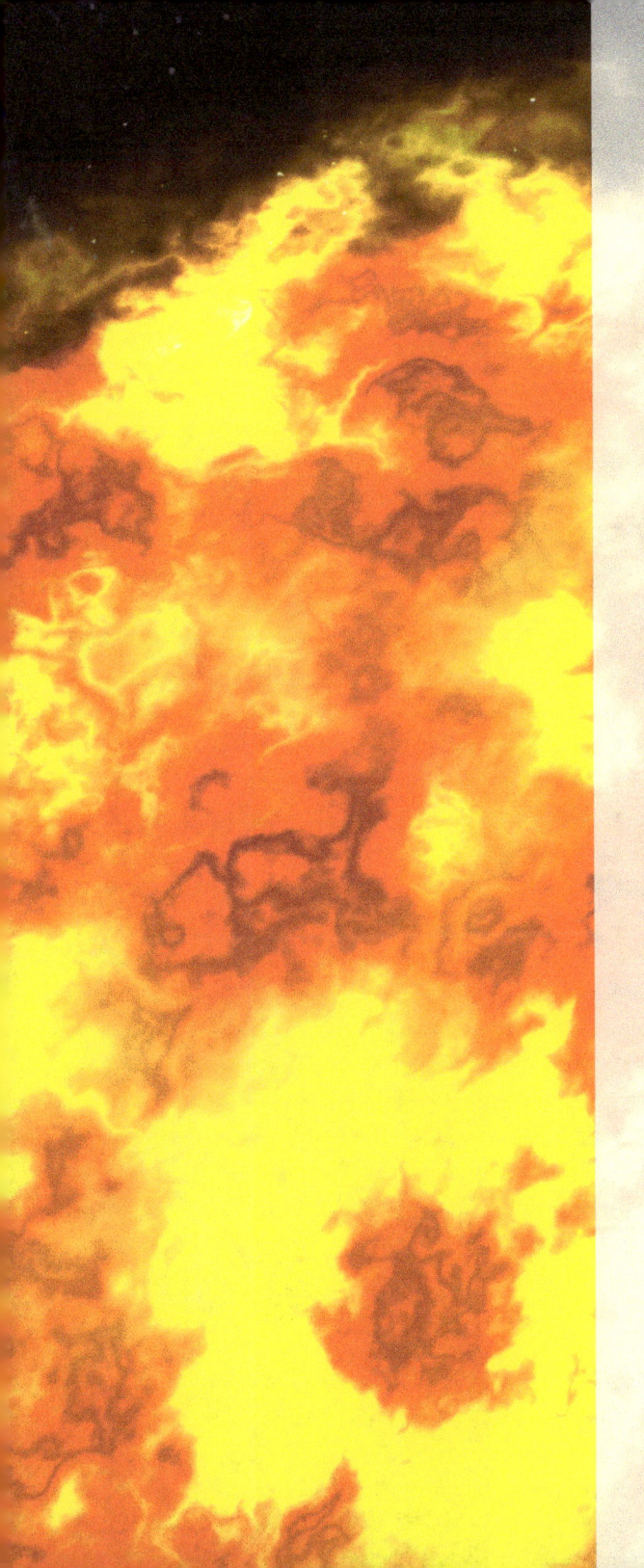

Most long-period comets are believed to originate from the Oort Cloud. They are considered long-period comets when they have orbital periods longer than 200 years.

The Oort Cloud contains many billions of comets, although some are very small. It is estimated that the total mass of the Oort Cloud's comets is 40 times the mass of Earth.

This cloud has a relatively dense core. It is near the ecliptic plane. It creates a steady state by replenishing the outer boundaries from the core.

Many wonders of our solar system are still waiting to be discovered. They are part of our wonderful and mysterious universe. By knowing them, we can appreciate that the universe is an infinite masterpiece. It is a masterpiece we are part of.

www.ingramcontent.com/pod-product-compliance
Lightning Source LLC
LaVergne TN
LVHW061321060426
835507LV00019B/2253